This COMPLETELY REVOLTING RECIPES

book belongs to:

COOK'S NOTES

These recipes are for the family to enjoy making together. Some could be dangerous without the help of an adult. Children, please have an adult with you when you are using knives, handling anything hot or using a food processor.

ROALD DAHL'S COMPLETELY REVOLTING RECIPES
A JONATHAN CAPE BOOK 978 0 224 08535 9

Published in Great Britain by Jonathan Cape,
an imprint of Random House Children's Books
A Random House Group Company

These recipes were previously published in *Roald Dahl's Revolting Recipes*, 1994,
and in *Roald Dahl's Even More Revolting Recipes*, 2001
First published as *Completely Revolting Recipes*, 2009
This edition published 2011

1 3 5 7 9 10 8 6 4 2

RECIPES DEVISED BY JOSIE FISON AND FELICITY DAHL:
*Strawberry Flavoured Chocolate Coated Fudge; Green Pea Soup; Wormy Spaghetti; Fresh Mudburgers;
Mosquitoes' Toes and Wampfish Roes Most Delicately Fried; Bunce's Doughnuts; George's Marvellous Medicine Chicken Soup;
Krokan Ice-Cream; Toffee Apples; Hot Frogs; Candy-Coated Pencils for Sucking in Class;
Hansel and Gretel Spare Ribs; Butterscotch; Peach Juice; Stink Bugs' Eggs; Bruce Bogtrotter's Cake; Scrambled Dregs;
Frobscottle; Crispy Wasp Stings on a Piece of Buttered Toast; Boggis's Chicken; Stickjaw for Talkative Parents;
Wonka's Nutty Crunch Surprise; Hot Ice-Cream for Cold Days; Hair Toffee to Make Hair Grow on Bald Men.*
RECIPES DEVISED BY LORI-ANN NEWMAN:
*The Royal Breakfast for Growing Giants; Hot-house Eggs; The Hotel Breakfast; Hornets Stewed in Tar;
Doc Spencer's Pie; Pishlets; Plushnuggets; Strawberry Bonbons; Tummyticklers; Boiled Slobbages;
Glumptious Globgobblers; Wonka's Whipple-Scrumptious Fudgemallow Delight; Grobswitchy Cake;
A Plate of Soil with Engine Oil; Luminous Lollies for Eating in Bed at Night; The Magic Green Crystal;
Nishnobblers; Butter Gumballs; Spitsizzlers; Sherbet Slurpers; Bean's Cider; Devil's Drenchers;
Liquid Chocolate Mixed by Waterfall; Fizzy Lifting Drinks; Blue Bubblers.*

Roald Dahl's
COMPLETELY REVOLTING RECIPES

Illustrated by
Quentin Blake

with photographs by Jan Baldwin
Recipes by Josie Fison, Lori-Ann Newman and Felicity Dahl

JONATHAN CAPE

CONTENTS

SUPER SLURPS

SPLENDIFEROUS MENU SUGGESTIONS

FASCINATING FOODIE FACTS

GLOSSARY

INTRODUCTION

Roald Dahl simply adored food. You only have to pick up one of his many books and, before long, there is some mention of a taste or a smell or some marvellous-sounding concoction which just has me licking my lips! All of which got me thinking. Why should only Farmer Bunce get to feast on delicious doughnuts? Why is only Willy Wonka allowed to make *Hot Ice-Cream for Cold Days*? And why, above all, do the gruesome Twits get to keep *Wormy Spaghetti* all to themselves? On second thoughts . . .

No, my point is that every Roald Dahl fan would love to nibble at the pages of their books and find they taste of *Plushnuggets* or *Sherbet Slurpers* or *Tummyticklers*. So, with the help of some great chefs, I came up with some truly disgusting . . . no, appalling . . . no, REVOLTING recipes to help you do just that! I think you'll find the results scrumdiddlyumptious!

Happy cooking!

Felicity Dahl, Gipsy House

USEFUL INFORMATION

Weights and Measures

All the recipes in this book have the ingredients specified in metric measurements, but it is very useful to know how to convert amounts into old-fashioned or imperial measurements as sometimes you will find them in other cookery books (belonging to old people such as your mums and dads!)

Weight conversion:

From	To	Multiply by
ounces	grams	28.35
grams	ounces	0.035
pounds	kilograms	0.45
kilograms	pounds	2.21
British tons	kilograms	1016
US tons	kilograms	907

Liquid conversion:

From	To	Multiply by
pints (20 fl oz)	litres	0.57
litres	pints (20 fl oz)	1.76
US pints (16 fl oz)	litres	0.47
litres	US pints	2.11
imperial gallons	litres	4.55
litres	imperial gallons	0.22

"Size, of course, was everything. Mr Hoppy chose all sorts of different sizes, some weighing only slightly more than Alfie's thirteen ounces, others a great deal more, but he didn't want any that weighed less."

from ESIO TROT

The Chef's Hat Classification:

"A man with a tall white hat who must have been the head chef shouted, 'Put the soup for the big party in the larger soup tureen!'"

from THE WITCHES

Each recipe has been graded with the Chef's Hat Classification to show you how easy or difficult it is. Please have a grown-up on hand when cooking all of these recipes and ask for help when using knives, a food processor or handling anything hot.

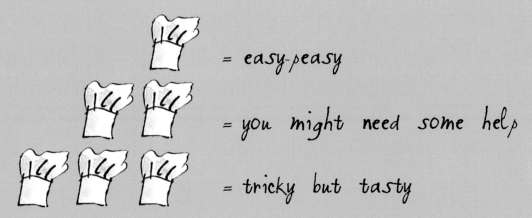

= easy-peasy

= you might need some help

= tricky but tasty

The glossary at the back of the book will help you with any ingredients you are not familiar with.

MARVELLOUS MUNCHES

I is a man-gobbling cannybull

'I is hungry!' the Giant boomed. He grinned, showing massive square teeth. The teeth were very white and very square and they sat in his mouth like huge slices of white bread.

'P . . . please don't eat me,' Sophie stammered.

The Giant let out a bellow of laughter. 'Just because I is a giant, you think I is a man-gobbling cannybull!' he shouted. 'You is about right! Giants is all cannybully and murderful! And they *does* gobble up human beans! We is in Giant Country now! Giants is everywhere around! Out there us has the famous Bonecrunching Giant! Bonecrunching Giant crunches up two whopsey whiffling human beans for supper every night! Noise is ear-bursting! Noise of crunching bones goes cracketycrack for miles around!'

'Owch!' Sophie said.

'Bonecrunching Giant only gobbles human beans from Turkey,' the Giant said. 'Every night Bonecruncher is galloping off to Turkey to gobble Turks.'

Sophie's sense of patriotism was suddenly so bruised by this remark that she became quite angry. 'Why Turks?' she blurted out. 'What's wrong with English?'

'Bonecrunching Giant says Turks is tasting oh ever so much juicier and more scrumdiddlyumptous! Bonecruncher says Turkish human beans has a glamourly flavour. He says Turks from Turkey is tasting of turkey.'

'I suppose they would,' Sophie said.

'Of course they would!' the Giant shouted. 'Every human bean is diddly different. Some is scrumdiddlyumptious and some is uckyslush. Greeks is all full of uckyslush. No giant is eating Greeks, ever.'

from THE BFG

Spitsizzlers

You will need:

2 saucepans
colander
paper towels
large slotted spoon
*an adult to assist with
the deep-frying*

200g vermicelli
oil
2 tsp (10ml) salt
2 tsp (10ml) mild curry powder

Perfect
birthday
party food

What you need to do:

1   Cook the vermicelli in boiling salted water for
5 minutes. Drain into a colander and then run
it under cold water to cool it down completely.
Pour a teaspoon of oil over it and mix with your
hands so that all the vermicelli is coated. This
is to stop it from sticking together.

2   Lay it out on a paper towel and cover it with
another layer of paper towel.

3   Pour oil into the saucepan until it is about 7cm
deep. Heat the oil so that it
is hot enough for a small
piece of vermicelli to sizzle
and float to the top if you
put it in.

4   Lay out more paper
towel ready next to the
saucepan you are
going to use to
deep-fry.

5   Mix together
the salt
and curry
powder
and set
aside.

"There were Gumtwizzlers and Fizzwinkles from China, Frothblowers and Spitsizzlers from Africa . . ."

6   Add a tangle of vermicelli to the oil. As soon as it hits the oil it will sizzle and spit and rise to the top. Carefully turn it over with the slotted spoon, leave for 1–2 minutes and then take out and place on the paper towel (it should not be brown, just stiff) and sprinkle with a large pinch of the salt and curry powder mix. Continue until all the vermicelli is used up.

Even better than crisps!

Crispy Wasp Stings on a Piece of Buttered Toast

You will need:

small round cutter
baking sheet
bowl

Buttered toast:

60g softened butter
½ tsp (2.5ml) cinnamon
4 slices of white bread

Wasp stings:

65g shredded coconut
25g icing sugar, sieved
3 tsp (15ml) clear honey/ golden syrup
grated zest of a ¼ of a lemon

Serves 16

Why not try on wholemeal bread?

Perfect birthday party food

What you need to do:

1   Work the butter and cinnamon together until thoroughly mixed.

2   Cut four discs out of each slice of bread and set aside.

3   Spread 50g shredded coconut onto a baking sheet and dredge with the sieved icing sugar.

4   Place under a hot grill until the sugar begins to caramelize (it will happen very quickly) then with a spatula turn over the coconut. Watch and repeat.

5   Place in a bowl and add the honey and lemon zest, and mix well.

6   Add the remaining coconut.

7   Toast the bread discs on both sides.

8   Spread with the cinnamon butter and top with the crispy wasp stings.

The Centipede's Song

'I've eaten many strange and scrumptious dishes in my time,
Like jellied gnats and dandyprats and earwigs cooked in slime,
And mice with rice – they're really nice
When roasted in their prime.
(But don't forget to sprinkle them with just a touch of grime.) . . .

'. . . I crave the tasty tentacles of octopi for tea
I like hot-dogs, I LOVE hot-frogs, and surely you'll agree
A plate of soil with engine oil's
A super recipe.
(I hardly need to mention that it's practically free.)

'For dinner on my birthday shall I tell you what I chose:
Hot noodles made from poodles and a slice of garden hose –
And a rather smelly jelly
Made from armadillo's toes.
(The jelly is delicious, but you have to hold your nose.)

'Now comes,' the Centipede declared, 'the burden of my speech:
These foods are rare beyond compare – some are right out of reach;
But there's no doubt I'd go without
A million plates of each
For one small mite,
One tiny bite,
Of this FANTASTIC PEACH!'

Tummyticklers

You will need:

1 massive frying pan
1 adult

3 soft flour tortillas
1 scant tbsp (15ml) grainy mustard
1 tbsp (15ml) mayonnaise
6 tbsp (90ml) grated Cheddar cheese
2 finely sliced spring onions
½ tbsp (7.5ml) olive oil
freshly ground black pepper

What you need to do:

1 Spread mustard over one tortilla and mayonnaise over the other.

2 Sprinkle both with cheese.

3 Scatter the spring onion over the one with mayonnaise. Stack one tortilla on top of the other and cover with the third tortilla.

4 Heat the massive frying pan, then add the oil.

5 Carefully transfer the stack of tortillas into the frying pan.

6 Cook on both sides over a medium heat until golden and crispy – about 2 minutes. An easy way of turning it over is to place a plate big enough to cover the whole thing over the frying pan and then turn everything upside down, so that you end up with it on the plate. Then slide it back into the pan so the other side can cook. Be careful when doing it as it is extremely hot.

7 Cut it into small slices like a cake and serve warm.

This won't make you itchy like a toe tickle – it's a delicate delight to soothe a hungry stomach. It's really like a toasted cheese stack, but don't stop at cheese – you can put in any fillings you like, even sweet ones, and you can have as many layers of tortillas in your Tummyticklers as your mouth can fit around. (This may require some training – nightly mouth-stretching.)

"There were . . . Tummyticklers and Gobwangles from the Fiji Islands and Liplickers and Plushnuggets from the land of the Midnight Sun."

Try serving with a tomato and basil salad

17

Stink Bugs' Eggs

You will need:

saucepan
bowl
sieve

4 eggs
3–4 brown outer onion skins
or 1 tbsp (15ml) food colouring
mayonnaise
salt and pepper
2 carrots, grated
1 carton of cress

Serves 4

What you need to do:

This needs to be made a day in advance and can be dyed naturally or with a food colouring.

1   Place eggs in a saucepan filled with water and bring to the boil.

2   Gently simmer for 10 minutes, take off the heat, cool in cold water (this is important) and then drain.

3   Carefully crack the shells all over with the back of a spoon.

"'I've eaten fresh mudburgers by the greatest cooks
there are, and scrambled dregs and stinkbugs' eggs
and hornets stewed in tar . . .'"

Natural colouring method:

4 Put the onion skins into the saucepan, lay the cracked, hard-boiled eggs
   on top and cover with water. Bring to the boil and simmer until the
   liquid is a deep brown colour, this takes approx. 1 hour. Remove from
   heat. Now follow step 5.

Food colouring method:

Place eggs in a bowl or glass, cover with water and add approx. 1 tbsp
of food colouring.

5 Leave to stand for at least eight hours or overnight before removing the
   shells.

6 Halve the eggs, press the yolks through a sieve, moisten them with a
   little mayonnaise.

7 The egg yolks can be mixed with a choice from the following; chopped
   ham, grated or cream cheese, chopped gherkins, Worcestershire sauce,
   curry powder, tomato sauce or cayenne pepper. Remember to season.

8 Replace the egg yolk mixture in the egg white halves and serve on a
   nest of grated carrot, and cress.

*NB. If you want to make the eggs
very smelly, sprinkle with
ready grated parmesan
cheese or asafoetida
(available from specialist
Indian shops), which
smells like sweaty
socks!*

Mosquitoes' Toes and Wampfish Roes Delicately Fried

You will need:

food processor
cling film
greaseproof paper
frying pan
kitchen paper

225g fresh cod fillet, de-boned
and skinned
2 tbsp (30ml) fresh ginger,
finely grated
10 spring onions, roughly chopped
½ tbsp (7.5ml) cornflour
salt and pepper
1 egg white
6–8 slices of bread (white or
wholemeal bread)
sesame and poppy seeds
oil for shallow frying

Makes 18–24

What you need to do:

These need to be refrigerated for 30 minutes before frying.

1   In a food processor quickly blend together cod, ginger, spring onions, cornflour and seasoning.

2   With the motor running add the egg until just combined.

3   Spread the paste thickly onto the bread slices.

4   Sprinkle generously with sesame and poppy seeds. Pat the seeds into the fish mixture with the flat side of a knife.

5   Cut off the breadcrusts and cut the slices of bread into 3 equal strips.

6   Place on a plate with a sheet of greaseproof paper between each layer. Cover with cling film. Place in fridge and leave for 30 minutes.

7   Heat a frying pan of oil until hot and fry the bread slices seed-side down until golden brown. Turn over and repeat.

8   Drain on kitchen paper before serving.

"'And have you ever tried
Mosquitoes' toes and wampfish roes
Most delicately fried?'"

Try with
mushy peas!

FABULOUS FEASTS

Secret plans and clever tricks!

The Enormous Crocodile grinned, showing hundreds of sharp white teeth. 'For my lunch today,' he said, 'I would like a nice juicy little child.'

'I never eat children,' the Notsobig One said. 'Only fish.'

'Ho, ho, ho!' cried the Enormous Crocodile. 'I'll bet if you saw a fat juicy little child paddling in the water over there at this very moment, you'd gulp him up in one gollop!'

'No, I wouldn't,' the Notsobig One said. 'Children are tough and chewy and nasty and bitter.'

'*Tough* and *chewy*!' cried the Enormous Crocodile. '*Nasty* and *bitter*! What awful tommy-rot you talk! They are juicy and yummy!'

'They taste so bitter,' the Notsobig One said, 'you have to cover them with sugar before you can eat them.'

'Children are bigger than fish,' said the Enormous Crocodile. 'You get bigger helpings.'

'You are greedy,' the Notsobig One said. 'You're the greediest croc in the whole river.'

'I'm the bravest croc in the whole river,' said the Enormous Crocodile. 'I'm the only one who dares to leave the water and go through the jungle to the town to look for little children to eat.'

'You've only done that once,' snorted the Notsobig One. 'And what happened then? They all saw you coming and ran away.'

'Ah, but today when I go, they won't see me at all,' said the Enormous Crocodile.

'Of course they'll see you,' the Notsobig One said. 'You're so enormous and ugly, they'll see you from miles away.'

The Enormous Crocodile grinned again, and his terrible sharp teeth sparkled like knives in the sun. 'Nobody will see me,' he said, 'because this time I've thought up secret plans and clever tricks.'

'*Clever tricks*?' cried the Notsobig One. 'You've never done anything clever in your life! You're the stupidest croc on the whole river!'

'I'm the cleverest croc on the whole river,' the Enormous Crocodile answered. 'For my lunch today I shall feast upon a fat juicy little child while you lie here in the river feeling hungry. Goodbye.'

from THE ENORMOUS CROCODILE

The Royal Breakfast for growing giants

You will need:

small frying pan
large appetite

1 tsp (5ml) oil
3 cocktail sausages
3 baby mushrooms
1 piece of back bacon, cut into strips
1 cherry tomato
3 quail eggs
1 piece of toast
butter

Makes 1

What you need to do:

1 Heat frying pan.

2 Add 1 tsp oil to warm pan.

3 Put sausages into pan and brown all over. When the sausages are nearly done, add the mushrooms and cook.

4 Add bacon to pan and cook to desired crispness.

5 Slice cherry tomato in half and add – cut side down – to pan. Cook for 2 minutes and carefully turn over.

6 Crack quail eggs into pan and fry until just cooked, but yolk is still soft (about 3 minutes).

7 Carefully slide everything onto a plate and eat immediately.

For a healthier breakfast, grill the sausages, bacon and tomatoes

Hot-house Eggs

You will need:

6cm pastry cutter
frying pan

1 slice of thickly cut bread
½ tbsp (7.5ml) oil
1 tbsp (15ml) butter
1 egg

What you need to do:

Use any type of egg for this recipe. If you are using an ostrich egg, the hole will need to be much bigger, but if you have a nematode egg, which is only 0.02mm, you will only need to make a pinprick in the bread.

1 Stamp out a hole in the bread with the pastry cutter.

2 Heat frying pan.

3 Add half the oil and butter to the pan.

4 When frothing add bread and cutout bit to pan.

5 Fry until golden brown and then flip over.

6 Carefully crack the egg into the hole and fry until cooked. If you like your eggs well done, you can flip the whole thing over and cook on the other side for about 30 seconds with the remaining butter and oil.

7 Serve with cutout bit.

Delumptious with whole fresh cherry tomatoes!

The Hotel Breakfast

"Breakfast was the best meal of the day in our hotel . . ."

You will need:

25cm non-stick frying pan with ovenproof handle or an ovenproof dish

6 rashers of smoked back bacon
5 eggs
salt and pepper
2 tbsp (30ml) milk

Serves 2

What you need to do:

1 Heat the oven to 200°C/gas mark 6.

2 Slice bacon.

3 Fry until it starts to crisp.

4 Mix eggs, salt, pepper and milk.

5 Add to pan. (If you are using an ovenproof dish, place all ingredients in the dish and place in the oven.)

6 Don't stir.

7 Leave on the heat for 1 minute.

8 Put in the oven until the whole thing is puffed up and golden on top (about 15 minutes).

9 Turn it out onto a plate and eat.

NB. If an ovenproof dish is used for this recipe, The Hotel Breakfast will take 20–25 minutes to cook in the oven.

The perfect holiday treat

Yummy with a big glass of freshly squeezed orange juice

from BOY

Scrambled Dregs

"'And scrambled dregs and stink bugs' eggs and hornets stewed in tar.'"

You will need:

saucepan

25g butter
2 eggs, lightly beaten
400g can of chicken consommé
salt and pepper

Serves 2

What you need to do:

1 Melt butter in a saucepan.

2 Add the egg and cook gently, stirring all the time until the egg is scrambled and dry.

3 Pour in the consommé and heat gently, up to boiling point.

4 Pour into soup bowls and allow to cool slightly before eating. Season to taste.

NB. You can dilute the consommé with water if you find the taste too strong.

Squiggly Spaghetti

The next day, to pay Mr Twit back for the frog trick, Mrs Twit sneaked out into the garden and dug up some worms. She chose big long ones and put them in a tin and carried the tin back to the house under her apron.

At one o'clock, she cooked spaghetti for lunch and she mixed the worms in with the spaghetti, but only on her husband's plate. The worms didn't show because everything was covered with tomato sauce and sprinkled with cheese.

'Hey, my spaghetti's moving!' cried Mr Twit, poking around in it with his fork.

'It's a new kind,' Mrs Twit said, taking a mouthful from her own plate which of course had no worms. 'It's called Squiggly Spaghetti. It's delicious. Eat it up while it's nice and hot.'

Mr Twit started eating, twisting the long tomato-covered strings around his fork and shovelling them into his mouth. Soon there was tomato sauce all over his hairy chin.

'It's not as good as the ordinary kind,' he said, talking with his mouth full. 'It's too squishy.'

'I find it very tasty,' Mrs Twit said. She was watching him from the other end of the table. It gave her great pleasure to watch him eating worms.

'I find it rather bitter,' Mr Twit said. 'It's got a distinctly bitter flavour. Buy the other kind next time.'

Mrs Twit waited until Mr Twit had eaten the whole plateful. Then she said, 'You want to know why your spaghetti was squishy?'

Mr Twit wiped the tomato sauce from his beard with a corner of the tablecloth. 'Why?' he said.

'And why it had a nasty bitter taste?'

'Why?'

'Because it was *worms*!' cried Mrs Twit, clapping her hands and stamping her feet on the floor and rocking with horrible laughter.

Wormy Spaghetti

Perfect for Halloween

You will need:

2 large saucepans
food processor

Sauce:

2 tbsp (30ml) sunflower oil
1 onion, chopped
2 sticks of celery, chopped
(optional)
1 clove of garlic, crushed
400g tin of plum tomatoes
1 tbsp (15ml) tomato purée
1 tbsp (15ml) parsley, chopped
1 bay leaf
1 tsp (5ml) sugar
2 carrots, grated
salt and pepper

2 tsp (10ml) olive oil
50g fusilli col buco spaghetti
(curly spaghetti)
225g tricolour spaghetti
(spinach, wholewheat and
ordinary)
170g Cheddar cheese (grated)

Serves 4–5

What you need to do:

1 Heat the oil in a saucepan and sweat the onion, celery (optional) and garlic until soft.

2 Add the remaining ingredients for the sauce *except* the carrot, bring to the boil and allow to simmer for 30 minutes.

3 Remove the bay leaf and liquidize the sauce until smooth.

4 Return the sauce to the saucepan, taste for seasoning and keep warm.

5 Meanwhile bring a large saucepan of water to the boil, add the olive oil and salt, long spaghetti and then fusilli broken into thirds and cook until tender. Drain.

6 Reheat the sauce and fold in the carrot until it is warm.

7 Divide out the spaghetti on each serving plate, spoon over the sauce and garnish with the grated cheese.

Serve with a tasty green salad!

Boggis's Chicken

You will need:

large saucepan
large casserole dish
measuring jug

1.6kg chicken
1 onion, sliced
450g carrots, peeled and sliced thickly
2 sticks of celery
a few parsley stalks
salt
peppercorns
bay leaf
1 chicken stock cube
150g frozen peas

Parsley sauce:
60g butter
60g flour
450ml milk
900ml chicken stock
6 tbsp (90ml) chopped parsley
salt and pepper

Dumplings:
100g self-raising flour
50g suet
50g sweetcorn (optional)
cold water to bind
salt and pepper

Serves 4–6

What you need to do:

1 Put the chicken into a large saucepan with all the ingredients except the peas.

2 Cover three quarters of the chicken with water.

3 Bring to the boil, reduce the heat and simmer gently for 1½ hours or until the chicken is cooked.

4 Remove the chicken from the saucepan and allow to cool. Strain the stock.

5 Pick out the carrots and put to one side.

6 Skim off all the fat from the stock and put 900ml into a measuring jug.

7 Remove the flesh from the chicken carcass, discard the skin and chop up.

The parsley sauce:

8 In an ovenproof casserole or a large saucepan, melt the butter and add the flour. Stir and cook for 1 minute.

9 Gradually add the combined milk and chicken stock. Bring to the boil stirring continuously for 1 minute and remove from the heat. Add 5½ tbsp parsley.

"Boggis was a chicken farmer. He kept thousands of chickens. He was enormously fat. This was because he ate three boiled chickens smothered with dumplings every day for breakfast, lunch and supper."

A perfect winter warmer

The dumplings:

10 Mix together the flour, suet, optional sweetcorn, and seasoning to taste. Bind with enough cold water to make a smooth dough. With floured hands, divide the dough into 12 portions and roll into balls.

11 Bring the sauce back to the simmer and add the chicken pieces, carrots, peas and the dumplings (they will sink, but don't worry).

12 Cover with a lid and allow to cook for about 20 minutes until the dumplings are light and fluffy.

13 Sprinkle with remaining parsley and serve.

NB. *As an alternative to dumplings, you can make molehills out of mashed potato.*

Glumptious Globgobblers

You will need:

saucepan
food processor
frying pan
1 adult
kitchen paper

125g Arborio rice
2 skinless and boneless
chicken breasts
1 tbsp (15ml) freshly grated ginger
1 tsp (5ml) medium curry powder
1 clove of garlic, crushed
3 tbsp (45ml) roughly chopped
coriander
4 spring onions, sliced
4 tbsp (60ml) sweetcorn
½ tsp (2.5ml) salt
freshly ground black pepper
100ml light soy sauce
oil for deep-frying

Makes 24

Yummy,
dipped in
hummus!

What you need to do:

The traditional globgobbler, made somewhere near Mecca, is a delicious sweet. This variety, made in a secret undercover location miles away from Mecca, is a mouth-watering savoury treat.

1   Cook rice in 450ml of boiling salted water for 15 minutes and then rinse under cold running water until completely cold.

2   Place chicken breasts in food processor and blitz until smooth.

3   Add all the other ingredients, apart from soy sauce and oil. Blitz again for about 30 seconds.

4   Heat oil – about 2cm deep – in a frying pan. This would be the moment for an adult to help out.

5   While the adult is assisting you in the deep-frying department, rub a bit of cold oil on your hands and grab a walnut-sized piece of the glumptious mix. Roll it into a ball. Continue until all the mixture is used up.

6   Stand back and hand over the globgobblers to the deep-frying department. The head of this department will then fry them until golden brown all over.

7   Drain on kitchen paper and sprinkle lightly with salt. Use soy sauce as a dip.

Perfect
birthday party
or picnic
food

"To the Giraffe I gave a bag of Glumptious Globgobblers. The Globgobbler is an especially delicious sweet that is made somewhere near Mecca, and the moment you bite into it, all the perfumed juices of Arabia go squirting down your gullet one after the other."

33

Doc Spencer's Pie

You will need:

pastry brush
baking sheet

4 slices of ham
4 hard-boiled eggs
1 tbsp (15ml) mayonnaise
*2 tbsp (30ml) grated
Cheddar cheese*
salt
freshly ground black pepper
1 pack filo pastry
40g butter, melted
sesame seeds

Makes 6

Perfect birthday party food

What you need to do:

Not exactly like Doc Spencer's wife makes for him, but easier to eat if you're stuck somewhere in the wild with no knife and can't find Mrs Doc Spencer.

1   Preheat the oven to 200°C/gas mark 6.

2   Roughly chop ham.

3   Roughly chop eggs.

4   Mix together ham, eggs, mayonnaise, Cheddar cheese, salt and pepper.

5   Cut a sheet of filo pastry in half widthways. Lay one piece on top of the other.

6   Brush with melted butter. Put 2 tbsp of egg and ham mix onto the pastry and carefully roll into a cigar shape, folding in the sides so that it is safely sealed.

7   Brush the top with melted butter and sprinkle with sesame seeds. Continue until all the mixture is used up, or you lose interest (the rest can be a delicious sandwich filling).

8   Bake in preheated oven for 15–20 minutes or until golden brown.

9   Allow to cool for 8 minutes before you eat it otherwise you'll burn your tongue.

"I saw before me the most enormous and beautiful pie in the world. It was covered all over, top, sides, and bottom, with a rich golden pastry."

from DANNY THE CHAMPION OF THE WORLD

Why not serve with boiled peas and sweetcorn?

Green Pea Soup

"Everyone in the big RSPCC party wants the soup!"

You will need:

2 large saucepans
food processor
sieve

25g butter
12 spring onions, roughly chopped
1 small potato, roughly diced
1 clove garlic, crushed
350g frozen peas
900ml chicken stock
salt and pepper

Garnish:

175g frozen peas
150ml double cream

Serves 4–5

What you need to do:

1 Melt the butter in a large saucepan.

2 Add the spring onions, potato and garlic.

3 Cover with a lid and sweat for 10 mins.

4 Add the peas, stock, salt and pepper, bring to the boil and simmer slowly for approx. 15 minutes.

5 Remove from the heat and liquidize.

6 Pass through a sieve into a clean saucepan.

7 Reheat adding the peas to garnish and cook until just tender. Add the cream and heat through, correcting the seasoning.

8. Serve in warm soup bowls with hot crusty bread.

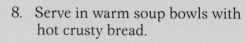

In the Kitchen

Higher and higher I swung. I was remembering the trapeze artist in the circus I had seen last Easter and the way he had got the trapeze swinging higher and higher and higher and had then let go and gone flying through the air. So just at the right moment, at the top of my swing, I let go with my tail and went soaring clear across the kitchen and made a perfect landing on the middle shelf!

By golly, I thought, what marvellous things a mouse can do! And I'm only a beginner!

No one had seen me. They were all far too busy with their pots and pans. From the middle shelf I somehow managed to shinny up a little water-pipe in the corner, and in no time at all I was up on the very top shelf just under the ceiling, among all the saucepans and the frying-pans. I knew that no one could possibly see me up there. It was a super position, and I began working my way along the shelf until I was directly above the big empty silver basin they were going to pour the soup into. I put down my bottle. I unscrewed the top and crept to the edge of the shelf and quickly poured what was in it straight into the silver basin below. The next moment, one of the cooks came along with a gigantic saucepan of steaming green soup and poured the whole lot into the silver basin. He put the lid on the basin and shouted, 'Soup for the big party all ready to go out!' Then the waiter arrived and carried the big silver basin away.

I had done it!

37

Fresh Mudburgers and Onion Rings

"I've eaten fresh mudburgers by the greatest cooks there are . . ."

You will need:

For the mudburgers:
mixing bowl
700g minced beef
1 medium onion, chopped
3 tbsp (45ml) tomato purée
2 tbsp (30ml) mild French mustard
1 tbsp (15ml) Worcestershire sauce
2–3tbsp (30–45ml) capers, drained
4 tbsp (60ml) fresh parsley, chopped
salt and pepper
1 egg, beaten

For the onion rings:
large polythene bag
1 onion
seasoned flour
vegetable oil

What to do:

Mudburgers:

1. In a mixing bowl break up the minced beef.

2. Add all the ingredients, except the egg, and gently mix together.

3. Add the egg, binding all the ingredients together and pat into mudburgers.

4. Preheat the grill and grill for 4–5 minutes on both sides or fry in a non-stick frying pan.

5. Serve in a bun with a 'revolting' relish. Cucumber relish is ideal!

Onion Rings:

1. Peel the onion and cut into 2–3mm thick slices, against the grain. Separate the rings.

2. Put them in a large polythene bag, containing seasoned flour, and shake until the rings are lightly coated with the flour, shake off any excess.

3. Deep-fry in hot oil until crispy and golden.

Hansel and Gretel Spare Ribs

Perfect for Halloween

from RHYME STEW

You will need:

roasting tin

675g American-style spare ribs
1 tbsp (15ml) Worcestershire sauce
1 tbsp (15ml) soy sauce
1 tbsp (15ml) English mustard
(Coleman's)
1 tbsp (15ml) tomato ketchup
1 tbsp (15ml) honey
1 medium onion, finely chopped
salt and pepper

Serves 4

NB. These must be well
cooked and crunchy, as
in the picture.

What you need to do:

1   Preheat the oven to 220°C/
gas mark 7.

2   Place the ribs in the roasting tin.

3   Mix all the remaining ingredients
together and with a knife paste the
ribs with the mixture.

4   Place the ribs in the oven and cook
for approx. 1½ hours turning every
half hour, and basting them with
the juices.

George's Marvellous Medicine Chicken Soup

You will need:

large saucepan

*2 small or 1 large corn-fed chicken
total 2.5kg (approx.)*

4 small onions

100g mushrooms

3 large carrots

2 leeks

*3 tsp (15ml) tarragon
(if fresh, chopped)*

salt and pepper

Serves 6

What you need to do:

*If you want to serve this for lunch you will
need to make it the day before.*

1   Quarter the chicken(s) and roughly
chop 2 onions. Place the chicken and
onions in a large saucepan and
cover with water.

2   Bring to the boil and simmer
until the liquid has reduced
by half. Skim the surface
when necessary. Top up
and reduce by half again.
This takes at least 4 hours.
Cool.

3   Strain and reserve the
liquid – you should have
approx. 1.5–1.75 litres.

"And suddenly, George found himself dancing around the steaming pot, chanting strange words that came into his head out of nowhere:"

4   Pick the meat off the bones, chop and set aside. If you have time, continue boiling the bones in fresh water, as in step 2, to add more flavour to the stock.

5   Chop remaining onions and other vegetables, add to the stock with the tarragon and cook until tender.

6   Season with salt and pepper to taste.

7   Before serving, add meat and heat through.

Perfect for lunch with your grandma

Boiled Slobbages

You will need:

large saucepan
large bowl
colander
spatula
frying pan

6 vine-ripened tomatoes
6 basil leaves
1 whole mozzarella cheese
4 tbsp (60ml) extra virgin olive oil
salt and pepper
2 eggs
130ml milk
¼ tsp (1.25ml) nutmeg
170g plain flour

Serves 3

What you need to do:

1   Chop tomatoes into small pieces.

2   Tear the basil leaves into small pieces.

3   Chop the mozzarella into small cubes.

4   Combine the tomato, mozzarella, basil, 3 tbsp of the olive oil, salt and pepper.

*"I often eat boiled slobbages.
They're grand when served beside
minced doodlebugs and curried slugs."*

5   Let this stand at room temperature for about an hour.

6   Meanwhile, mix together eggs, milk, salt, pepper and freshly grated nutmeg.

7   Add the flour to the egg mixture. If it appears lumpy, use a whisk.

8   Let it rest in the fridge for 10 minutes.

9   Put a large pan of salted water on to boil.

10 Fill a large bowl with cold water.

11 When the water in the pan is boiling, hold the colander above the saucepan and pour the mixture into it, pushing it through with a spatula.

12 Simmer the slobbages for 2 minutes and then remove them with a slotted spoon and put them straight into the bowl of cold water.

13 When you are ready to eat, drain the slobbages and heat them in a frying pan with the remaining olive oil.

14   Add the tomato sauce, stir and serve.

*N.B. The sauce needs to be prepared an hour
ahead, and the slobbages can be prepared a few
hours ahead and then reheated when you are
ready to eat.*

A rare delicacy – by far the best slobbages in the land.

TONGUE-TICKLINGLY TASTY SWEET TREATS

The most wonderful
sweet shop in the world!

'There is an old wooden house near where I live,' I said. 'It's called The Grubber and long ago it used to be a sweet shop. I have wished and wished that one day somebody might come along and make it into a marvellous new sweet shop all over again.'

'Somebody?' cried the Duke. 'What do you mean, somebody? You and I will do that! We'll do it together! We'll make it into the most wonderful sweet shop in the world! And *you*, my boy, will own it!'

Whenever the old Duke got excited, his moustaches started to bristle and jump about. Right now they were jumping up and down so much it looked as though he had a squirrel on his face. 'By Gad, sir!' he cried, waving his stick. 'I shall buy the place today! Then we'll get to work and we'll have the whole thing ready in no time! You just wait and see what sort of a sweet shop we are going to make out of this Grubber place of yours!'

It was amazing how quickly things started to happen after that. There was no problem about buying the house because it was owned by the Giraffe and the Pelly and the Monkey, and they insisted upon giving it to the Duke for nothing.

Then the builders and carpenters moved in and rebuilt the whole of the inside so that once again it had three floors. On all these floors they put together rows and rows of tall shelves, and there were ladders to climb up to the highest shelves and baskets to carry what you bought.

Then the sweets and chocs and toffees and fudges and nougats began pouring in to fill the shelves. They came by aeroplane from every country in the world, the most wild and wondrous things you could ever imagine.

from THE GIRAFFE AND THE PELLY AND ME

45

Nishnobblers

You will need:

pyrex bowl
saucepan
30x25cm sheet of bubble wrap
7cm pastry cutter
pastry brush

100g good quality dark
chocolate
100g good quality white
cooking chocolate

Makes 6

Yummy
with a big
glass of
milk!

What you need to do:

Nishnobblers are made from tempered chocolate. Tempering is when you mix melted and solid chocolate together to make it shiner and more manageable. It is an indispensable skill to have in life, and you learn how to do it right here! Once you've got the hang of it, you'll be able to create masterful chocolate constructions to rival Willy Wonka's.

1   Melt 70g of the dark chcoclate in a pyrex bowl on the defrost setting in the microwave or over a saucepan of simmering water. When it is melted, stir the unmelted 30g into it until the whole lot is smooth.

"... there were Nishnobblers and Gumglotters and Blue Bubblers and Sherbet Slurpers and Tongue Rakers, and as well as all this, there was a whole lot of splendid stuff from the great Wonka factory itself."

from THE GIRAFFE AND THE PELLY AND ME

2 Paint over the bubble wrap with the melted chocolate and place it in the fridge for 15 minutes.

3 Temper the white chocolate in the same way (NB. White chocolate melts faster than dark chocolate, so you may want to let it cool a little before you start painting.) Spread it over the dark chocolate. Chill for 15 minutes.

4 Carefully peel the bubble wrap away from the chocolate and cut it into rounds with the pastry cutter.

A perfect birthday party treat

Hair Toffee to Make Hair Grow on Bald Men

(for mums to make only)

You will need:

large saucepan
small greased tin or tray
sugar thermometer
cellophane, foil or greaseproof paper

50g unsalted butter
225g granulated sugar
1 tbsp (15ml) warm water
1 tbsp (15ml) white wine vinegar
2 tbsp (30ml) golden syrup
100g egg vermicelli, broken in half and cooked

A super present (not just for bald people!)

What you need to do:

1. Melt the butter in a large, heavy-bottomed pan, stir in the sugar and remove the pan from the heat.

2. Add the water, vinegar and syrup and stir over a low heat until the sugar dissolves. DO NOT allow the mixture to boil.

3. Add the egg vermicelli.

4. Place the sugar thermometer into the pan.

5. Now bring the mixture to boiling point and boil steadily for approx. 15–20 minutes until the thermometer reads 152°C.

6. Pour the toffee into the greased tin and allow to cool. As soon as it is cool enough to handle, lightly grease your hands with butter. Take two forks and scrape up a few strands of vermicelli. Then using your hands, roll the toffee into a small bite-sized mound. Repeat.

7. Place on greased tray and allow to set.

8. Wrap and twist individually in greaseproof paper, kitchen foil or, better still, cellophane, to prevent them from becoming sticky.

Toffee Apples

"Quickly, Charlie started reading some of the labels alongside the buttons . . . TOFFEE-APPLE TREES FOR PLANTING OUT IN YOUR GARDEN - ALL SIZES."

You will need:

melon-scoop
orange sticks (available at chemists) or cocktail sticks
small saucepan
sugar thermometer

20cm bowl containing water and ice cubes
4 eating apples
½ tbsp (7.5ml) water
100g caster sugar
25g butter

Serves 4

What you need to do:

These need to be made at the last moment because they will start to "weep" after an hour.

1 Using the melon-scoop, scoop as many balls as possible from 3 apples. Each apple ball must have some skin on it.

2 Place an orange stick or cocktail stick into the remaining skin left on each ball.

3 Place all the ingredients into a saucepan and heat gently, stirring occasionally. Turn up the heat and boil to 160°C. The mixture will become a deep chestnut brown. Turn off the heat and allow bubbles to subside.

4 Remove bowl of iced water from the fridge. Working as quickly as possible, dip the apples into the toffee one at a time. Rotate a few times to get an even coating and drop into the iced water for approx. 30 seconds.

5 Now stick the baby toffee apples into the remaining whole apple and continue until all the toffee is used up.

49

Butter Gumballs

You will need:

medium-size heavy-bottomed saucepan
friends with strong arms
large tray
non-stick baking parchment
tin foil
plenty of time

1 tin condensed milk
2 tbsp (30ml) demerara sugar
2 tbsp (30ml) golden syrup
30g butter

What you need to do:

1   Put all the ingredients into the saucepan and stir over a low heat until it becomes a beautiful toffee colour, and quite thick. This will take about 25–30 minutes, and it is important that you stir for the whole time, otherwise it will burn at the bottom.

2   Cover a large tray with non-stick baking parchment, and using 2 teaspoons, put teaspoon-sized blobs of the mixture onto the paper, spaced well apart.

"The sweet-shop of my dreams would be loaded from top to bottom with Sherbet Suckers and Caramel Fudge and Russian Toffee and Sugar Snorters and Butter Gumballs and thousands and thousands of other glorious things like that."

from THE GIRAFFE AND THE PELLY AND ME

A perfect birthday party treat

3   Allow the blobs to get completely cold and then shape into balls by rubbing them between your palms. If the mixture doesn't stay in shape it means that it needs to be cooked for a little longer, so head back to the stove and start stirring.

4   If you are going to give a few away as presents then cut squares of tin foil and wrap each Butter Gumball up like a Christmas cracker.

These make great presents for parents, as they can't talk for ages while they chew and chew and chew. The recipe makes enough for you to keep a small supply for yourself as well.

Wonka's Nutty Crunch Surprise

You will need:

pyrex bowl
saucepan
20x25cm shallow tin, greased
and lined with greaseproof paper
greaseproof paper

200g plain chocolate, broken
into small pieces
50g butter
5 tbsp (75ml) golden syrup
165g Rich Tea biscuits,
finely crushed
75g flaked almonds
25g Rice Crispies
a few drops of vanilla essence

For the nutty crunch:

50g flaked almonds,
finely chopped
100g granulated sugar
2 tbsp (30ml) water

For the chocolate coating:

200g milk chocolate, broken
into small pieces

What you need to do:

1 Put the chocolate, butter and golden syrup in a pyrex bowl and place over a saucepan of simmering water. Stir occasionally until melted. Alternatively place in microwave oven and cook on high for 1½ minutes.

2 Add the almonds, crushed biscuits, Rice Crispies and vanilla essence and mix well.

3 Spoon the mixture into the lined tin and press down firmly with the back of a fork, creating a level surface.

4 Allow to cool in the fridge, and then cut into bars.

5 Then make the nutty crunch: begin by placing the water and sugar into a small saucepan. Leave on a low heat until the sugar has dissolved. Do not stir, but occasionally swirl the pan around gently. Increase the heat and continue stirring until the sugar caramelizes and turns golden brown, approx. 2–3 minutes.

A perfect birthday party treat

"'Have you got it?' whispered Grandpa George, his eyes shining with excitement. Charlie nodded and held out the bar of chocolate. WONKA'S NUTTY CRUNCH SURPRISE, it said on the wrapper."

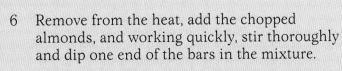

6 Remove from the heat, add the chopped almonds, and working quickly, stir thoroughly and dip one end of the bars in the mixture.

7 Melt the chocolate in the pyrex bowl, over a saucepan of simmering water, or microwave. Once it has melted, remove from the heat and dip the opposite end of each bar in the chocolate.

8 Leave to cool on a sheet of greaseproof paper.

Bunce's Doughnuts

You will need:

cling film

*2 plain round cutters
(3cm and 6cm)*

kitchen paper

small bowl

100g soft brown sugar

50g unsalted butter

1 egg

450g plain flour

½ tbsp (7.5ml) baking powder

½ tsp (2.5ml) cinnamon

a good pinch of salt

2 tbsp (30ml) hot water

¼ tsp (1.25ml) vanilla essence

75ml milk

vegetable oil for deep frying

caster sugar for coating

Makes 12–14

What you need to do:

These are best eaten warm. The dough needs to be made and refrigerated for 2 hours or overnight before cooking.

1 Cream the sugar and butter until pale and creamy – this can be done using a food processor.

2 Gradually add the egg until blended.

3 Add the remaining ingredients. The dough should be fairly stiff but smooth.

4 Wrap in cling-film and refrigerate for 2 hours.

5 Divide the dough in half and replace the other half in the fridge.

6 On a floured surface roll out the dough to 0.5cm thickness. With the cutters cut out as many doughnuts as possible.

7 Gather up all the scraps, roll and cut as many additional doughnuts as possible and repeat with the remaining dough.

8 Heat the vegetable oil up to 190°C until it is sizzling.

"His food was doughnuts and goose-livers. He mashed the livers into a disgusting paste and then stuffed the paste into the doughnuts. This diet gave him a tummy-ache and a beastly temper."

from FANTASTIC MR FOX

9 Fry the doughnuts in small batches turning once until golden brown.

10 Drain on absorbent kitchen paper.

11 Place the sugar in the bowl and add a few doughnuts at a time, shaking them in the sugar until coated.

12 Serve immediately.

Share with friends to avoid bellyache!

Bruce Bogtrotter
and the Cake

'There you are, cook,' the Trunchbull cried. 'Bogtrotter likes your cake. He adores your cake. Do you have any more of your cake you could give him?'

'I do indeed,' the cook said. She seemed to have learned her lines by heart.

'Then go and get it. And bring a knife to cut it with.'

'The cook disappeared. Almost at once she was back again staggering under the weight of an enormous round chocolate cake on a china platter. The cake was fully eighteen inches in diameter and it was covered with dark-brown chocolate icing. 'Put it on the table,' the Trunchbull said . . .

. . . The cook stood there like a shrivelled bootlace, tight-lipped, implacable, disapproving. She looked as though her mouth was full of lemon juice.

'Come on then,' the Trunchbull said. 'Why don't you cut yourself a nice thick slice and try it?'

'What? Now?' the boy said, cautious. He knew there was a catch in this somewhere, but he wasn't sure where. 'Can't I take it home instead?' he asked.

'That would be impolite,' the Trunchbull said, with a crafty grin. 'You must show cookie here how grateful you are for all the trouble she's taken.'

The boy didn't move.

'Go on, get on with it,' the Trunchbull said. 'Cut a slice and taste it. We haven't got all day . . .'

. . . As the very last mouthful disappeared, a tremendous cheer rose up from the audience and the children were leaping on their chairs and yelling and clapping and shouting, 'Well done, Brucie! Good for you, Brucie! You've won a gold medal, Brucie!'

The Trunchbull stood motionless on the platform. Her great horsy face had turned the colour of molten lava and her eyes were glittering with fury. She glared at Bruce Bogtrotter who was sitting on his chair like some huge overstuffed grub, replete, comatose, unable to move or speak. A fine sweat was beading his forehead but there was a grin of triumph on his face.

Suddenly the Trunchbull lunged forward and grabbed the large empty china platter on which the cake had rested. She raised it high in the air and brought it down with a crash right on the top of the wretched Bruce Bogtrotter's head and pieces flew all over the platform.

The boy was by now so full of cake he was like a sackful of wet cement and you couldn't have hurt him with a sledge-hammer. He simply shook his head a few times and went on grinning.

'Go to blazes!' screamed the Trunchbull as she marched off the platform followed closely by the cook.

Bruce Bogtrotter's

You will need:

20cm cake tin
greaseproof paper
pyrex bowl
saucepan
skewer
wire rack
palette knife

225g good quality
plain chocolate
175g unsalted butter, softened
225g caster sugar
4 tbsp (60ml) plain flour
6 eggs, separated

Coating:
225g good quality
plain chocolate
225g double cream

Serves 1–8!

What you need to do:

1. Preheat oven to 180°C/gas mark 4.

2. Grease and line the cake tin with greaseproof paper.

3. Melt the chocolate in a pyrex bowl, over a saucepan of simmering water or on a low heat in a microwave.

4. Mix in the butter and stir until melted.

5. Add the flour, sugar and lightly beaten egg yolks.

6. Whisk the egg whites until stiff.

7. Gently fold half of the whites into the chocolate mixture, mixing thoroughly.

8. Then carefully fold in the remaining whites.

For a slighty healthier option, serve without the coating

Cake

"Come here cook! Bogtrotter wishes to tell you how good your chocolate cake is!"

9   Cook for approx. 35 minutes. There will be a thin crust on top of the cake, and if tested with a skewer the inside will appear insufficiently cooked but don't worry as this is the character of the cake and it gets firmer as it cools. This cake is deliciously moist and light.

10 Leave to cool in the tin on a wire rack.

11 When cool enough to handle remove from the cake tin and discard the greaseproof paper.

12 In a pyrex bowl over a saucepan of simmering water melt together the chocolate and cream, stirring occasionally until the chocolate is fully melted and blended with the cream.

13 Allow to cool slightly.

14 The cake is prone to sinking slightly in the middle so place upside down for coating.

15 With a palette knife spread the chocolate coating all over the cake.

16 Allow to set in a cool place before serving.

The best ever birthday cake

59

Sherbet Slurpers

You will need:

5 plastic straws
1 lighter
1 adult
1 piece of paper

½ tsp (2.5ml) citric acid
(available from chemists)
4 Lucozade glucose energy
tablets, crushed to a
fine powder
¼ tsp (1.25ml) bicarbonate of soda
1–2 tsp (5–10ml) of icing sugar

Makes 5

What you need to do:

You might want to put on your laboratory coat for this recipe – it's more of a chemistry process than a cooking one! Once the mixture is made it is scooped into straws, which are then sealed – the perfect size to stash in a pocket for an emergency slurp . . .

1   Ask an adult to seal the end of all the straws by melting one end of the straw and then pressing it together with his/her fingers. The plastic does get hot, so the lighter should be held to it for just a couple of seconds before the edges are pressed together.

"... there were Nishnobblers and Gumglotters and Blue Bubblers and Sherbet Slurpers and Tongue Rakers, and as well as all this, there was a whole lot of splendid stuff from the great Wonka factory itself."

2   Mix together the first 3 ingredients and then add 1 tsp of the icing sugar. Taste it before you add more, as this may already be sweet enough for you. Don't add too much, as the fizz will disappear.

3   Fold a large piece of paper and then pour the Slurper mix into the fold. Get it into the straw by scooping the straw along through the mix and tapping the sealed end on the surface you're working on between each scoop.

4   As each one is filled, ask the adult to seal the other end in the same way as before. When you are ready to slurp your sherbet, open up one end of the straw and insert into mouth.

A perfect birthday party or picnic treat

Hornets Stewed in Tar

You will need:

baking sheet
roasting tin
saucepan
1 adult

375g mixed seeds –
pumpkin seeds, sunflower
seeds, sesame seeds, poppy
seeds and pine nuts
(all shucked)
500g granulated sugar
375ml water
juice of ½ a lemon
1 tbsp (15ml) black
food colouring

What you need to do:

1 Toast the seeds (apart from the poppy
   seeds) on a baking sheet in a 200°C/gas
   mark 6 oven for 10 minutes. Allow to cool.

2 Lightly butter the roasting tin and set
   to one side.

3 Put sugar and water in a saucepan over
   a low heat and stir until all the sugar
   has dissolved.

4   Turn the heat up and stop stirring. Be very careful, as boiling sugar is extremely hot. Stand back from the saucepan, but don't leave the kitchen because caramel always burns if you turn your back on it.

5   When it starts turning a beautiful golden colour (about 10 minutes), add the lemon juice and food colouring. Add it quickly and then move your hand away immediately, as it will spit and splutter like a live volcano.

6   Quickly stir in all the seeds and pour into the roasting tin. Leave to cool and harden. When it is completely cold, turn it out and break it into bite-size chunks. Keep them in an airtight container and they will remain delicious for days.

A super present

Put some in your lunchbox as a special treat!

63

Plushnuggets

You will need:

7cm pastry cutter
rolling pin
pastry brush
baking tray

2 bananas
2 tsp (10ml) maple syrup
2 tsp (10ml) olive oil
1 pack puff pastry
(preferably all butter)
1 egg yolk

Makes 12

What you need to do:

1 Squish the bananas with a fork and add maple syrup and olive oil.

2 Cut a 7cm-wide circle out of the pastry with a pastry cutter.

3 Roll the circle out so it is 1.5cm bigger.

4 Put a blob of the banana mix in the middle and lift up the edges to squash them together.

5 Use up the rest of the pastry in the same way.

"There were Gumtwizzlers and Fizzwinkles from China Frothblowers and Spitsizzlers from Africa, Tummyticklers and Gobwangles from the Fiji Islands and Liplickers and Plushnuggets from the land of the Midnight Sun."

6   Put in the fridge.

7   Heat oven to 200°C/gas mark 6.

8   When oven is at correct temperature, brush plushnuggets with yolk and put in the oven on the baking tray for about 20 minutes or until they are golden.

9   Allow them to cool for about 10 minutes before you eat them, as the middle remains very hot.

Candy-coated Pencils for

You will need:

medium saucepan

sugar thermometer

*20x25cm baking tin,
greased and lined with
greaseproof paper*

buttered knife

6 pencils

*Playdoh, plasticine or oasis
(available from florists)*

225g cube sugar

150ml water

*a good pinch of
cream of tartar*

*a few drops of flavourings
or colourings*

Makes 6

What you need to do:

1   Put the sugar and water in a saucepan over a gentle heat and stir until sugar has dissolved.

2   Raise the heat and when it's almost boiling add the cream of tartar and the sugar thermometer.

3   Boil without stirring to 121°C.

4   Remove from the heat and add flavouring and colouring. Do not over stir and *be very careful* as the mixture is extremely hot.

N.B. Do not double the recipe to make more, instead make in several batches.

Sucking in Class

5   Pour the mixture into the lined baking tin. The edges of the mixture will cool more quickly than the centre so, as the mixture cools, turn the edges inwards with a buttered knife, but do not stir.

6   Working quickly, lay two thirds of a pencil onto the mixture. Lift up and gently turn the candy around the pencil. You can create all kinds of shapes but make sure the candy is almost completely set before you stand your pencils in the Playdoh, plasticine or oasis.

7   Try not to put your fingers on the candy coating as you will leave your fingerprints behind.

8   Repeat this with the other pencils.

The Magic Green Crystal

You will need:

small saucepan
1 adult
baking tray, oiled

80g caster sugar
2 tbsp (30ml) golden syrup
1 tbsp (15ml) lemon juice
3 tbsp (45ml) water
½ tbsp (7.5ml) green
food colouring
1 tsp (5ml) bicarbonate of soda

What you need to do:

Warning! These sacred treasures will be much in demand. Don't leave home without securing your lunchbox with an alarm and a padlock. You can never be too careful when it comes to the magic green crystal.

1   Put the sugar, syrup, lemon juice and 3 tbsp water into the saucepan. Start it on a low heat and stir until all the sugar has dissolved.

2   Turn the heat up and boil without stirring until it is a rich golden caramel brown (about 10 minutes).

"'Take a look, my dear,' he said, opening the bag and tilting it towards James. Inside it, James could see a mass of tiny green things that looked like little stones or crystals."

3   Remove from the heat and quickly stir in the food colouring and then the bicarbonate of soda – it will froth up straight away.

4   Pour it onto the oiled baking tray and let it start to set.

5   Just before it hardens completely, cut into diamonds with an oiled knife.

A super present

Hot Ice-Cream for Cold Days

You will need:

ovenproof dish
25cm wide x 5cm deep

1 Jamaica ginger cake

420g tin peach slices

1 litre ice-cream (you
probably won't use all of this)

stem ginger in syrup,
drained and chopped finely
(as little or as much as you dare)

3 egg whites

a pinch of salt

175g caster sugar

Serves 6

What you need to do:

1 Preheat oven to 230°C/gas mark 8.

2 Whisk the egg whites with the salt to a stiff snow. Gradually whisk in the sugar until the meringue is very thick and shiny.

3 Cut the Jamaica ginger cake into 3 horizontal slices. Then cut each slice into a third again.

4 Brush each slice with a little peach syrup.

5 Arrange the 9 slices to roughly form a cube in the ovenproof dish.

6 Divide the peaches equally and arrange on top of the cake.

A perfect winter warmer

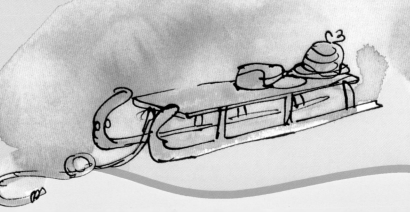

"'Extremely useful in the winter,' said Mr Wonka. 'Hot ice cream warms you up no end in freezing weather ...'"

7   Mix the chopped slices of stem ginger into the meringue.

8   Carefully scoop the ice-cream on top of the peaches.

9   Spoon the meringue over the ice-cream, enclosing the cake.

10   Place the pudding in the oven until it has turned golden brown (approx 3–5 minutes).

NB. If you want to add a frisson of excitement to the occasion you can warm up a little brandy in a ladle, set it alight and pour over the pudding.

Serve immediately.

Augustus Gloop goes up the pipe

'He's disappeared!' yelled Mrs Gloop. 'Where does that pipe go to? Quick! Call the fire brigade!'

'Keep calm!' cried Mr Wonka. 'Keep calm, my dear lady, keep calm. There is no danger! No danger whatsoever! Augustus has gone on a little journey, that's all. A most interesting little journey. But he'll come out of it just fine, you wait and see.'

'How can he possibly come out just fine?' snapped Mrs Gloop. 'He'll be made into marshmallows in five seconds!'

'Impossible!' cried Mr Wonka. 'Unthinkable! Inconceivable! Absurd! He could never be made into marshmallows!'

'And why not, may I ask?' shouted Mrs Gloop.

'Because that pipe doesn't go anywhere near it! That pipe – the one Augustus went up – happens to lead directly to the room where I make a most delicious kind of strawberry-flavoured chocolate-coated fudge . . .'

'Then he'll be made into strawberry-flavoured chocolate-coated fudge!' screamed Mrs Gloop. 'My poor Augustus! They'll be selling him by the pound all over the country tomorrow morning!'

'Quite right,' said Mr Gloop.

'I *know* I'm right,' said Mrs Gloop.

'It's beyond a joke,' said Mr Gloop.

'Mr Wonka doesn't seem to think so!' cried Mrs Gloop. 'Just look at him! He's laughing his head off! How *dare* you laugh like that when my boy's just gone up the pipe! You monster!' she shrieked, pointing her umbrella at Mr Wonka as though she was going to run him through. 'You think this is a joke, do you? You think that sucking my boy up into your Fudge Room like that is just one great big colossal joke?'

'He'll be perfectly safe,' said Mr Wonka, giggling slightly.

'He'll be chocolate fudge!' shrieked Mrs Gloop.

'Never!' cried Mr Wonka.

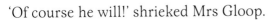

'Of course he will!' shrieked Mrs Gloop.

'I wouldn't allow it!' cried Mr Wonka.

'And why not?' shrieked Mrs Gloop.

'Because the taste would be terrible,' said Mr Wonka. 'Just imagine it! Augustus-flavoured chocolate-coated Gloop! No one would buy it!'

'They most certainly would!' cried Mr Gloop indignantly.

'I don't want to think about it!' shrieked Mrs Gloop.

'Nor do I,' said Mr Wonka. 'And I do promise you, madam, that your darling boy is perfectly safe.'

'If he is perfectly safe, then where is he?' snapped Mrs Gloop. 'Lead me to him this instant!'

Mr Wonka turned around and clicked his fingers sharply, *click, click, click*, three times. Immediately, an Oompa-Loompa appeared, as if from nowhere, and stood beside him.

The Oompa-Loompa bowed and smiled, showing beautiful white teeth. His skin was rosy-white, his long hair was golden-brown, and the top of his head came just above the height of Mr Wonka's knee. He wore the usual deerskin slung over his shoulder.

'Now listen to me!' said Mr Wonka, looking down at the tiny man, 'I want you to take Mr and Mrs Gloop up to the Fudge Room and help them to find their son, Augustus. He's just gone up the pipe.'

The Oompa-Loompa took one look at Mrs Gloop and exploded into peals of laughter.

'Oh, do be quiet!' said Mr Wonka. 'Control yourself! Pull yourself together! Mrs Gloop doesn't think it's all that funny!'

'You can say that again!' said Mrs Gloop.

'Go straight to the Fudge Room,' Mr Wonka said to the Oompa-Loompa, 'and when you get there, take a long stick and start poking around inside the big chocolate-mixing barrel. I'm almost certain you'll find him in there. But you'd better look sharp! You'll have to hurry! If you leave him in the chocolate-mixing barrel too long, he's liable to get poured out into the fudge boiler, and that really *would* be a disaster, wouldn't it? My fudge would become *quite* uneatable!'

Strawberry Flavoured Chocolate Coated Fudge

You will need:

20x25cm shallow baking tin
greaseproof paper
large saucepan
sugar thermometer
cutters

450g caster sugar
100g unsalted butter
175ml evaporated milk
a few generous drops of pink food colouring
a generous ½ tsp (2.5ml) of strawberry food flavouring (Supercook)
100g melted chocolate for dipping

Makes enough for 10 greedy children

What you need to do:

1 Line the tin with buttered greaseproof paper.

2 Put all the ingredients except flavouring and colouring into a large heavy-bottomed saucepan and place over a low heat.

3   Stir occasionally. Once the sugar has dissolved, gently boil the mixture and now stir all the time (to prevent sticking and burning on the bottom of the pan). Place the sugar thermometer into the saucepan and boil to soft ball (118°C). This takes about 5 minutes.

4   Take the pan off the heat, stir until the bubbles subside and then add the flavouring and the colouring.

5   Beat rapidly with a wooden spoon until the mixture thickens and becomes granular, approx. 3 minutes.

6   Pour the fudge into the lined tin and leave to set. If necessary, smooth with a palette knife dipped into boiling water.

7   With shaped cutters, cut the fudge and dip one side into the melted chocolate; or decorate with piped chocolate, creating different patterns as in illustration.

A super present

Pishlets

You will need:

shallow roasting tin
saucepan

170g butter
150g demerara sugar
1 tsp (5ml) bicarbonate of soda
1 apple
1 pear
200g oats
75g raisins
75g dried cherries

What you need to do:

You know that enormously annoying feeling when you know you want to eat something, and you rack your brains but still can't decide? Next time this feeling strikes you down, don't stop to think, just run into the kitchen without delay, and make up a batch of Pishlets.

1   Grease a shallow roasting tin.

2   Heat the oven to 180°C/gas mark 4.

3   Melt the butter, Demerara sugar and bicarbonate of soda in a saucepan on a low heat.

"They had a splendid effect upon the pelican, for after he had put one of them into his beak and chewed it for a while, he suddenly started singing like a nightingale."

4   While they are melting, peel the apple and pear and chop them into bite-sized chunks.

5   Add the oats, raisins, dried cherries, apple and pear to the saucepan and mix well.

6   Spoon into the roasting tin and spread evenly.

7   Place in the oven and cook for 25–30 minutes until golden on top.

8   Let it cool down and then cut it into squares.

A perfect birthday party or picnic treat

A Plate of Soil with Engine Oil

You will need:

2lb loaf tin
mixing bowl
shallow roasting tin
deep serving dish

170g plain flour
150g soft brown sugar
50g cocoa powder
150ml milk
50g butter, melted
100g dark chocolate
55g soft brown sugar
400ml hot milk
cream

Serves 6

What you need to do:

1   Grease the loaf tin.

2   Preheat the oven to 180°C/gas 4.

3   Mix the flour and the first amount of sugar with half the cocoa powder.

4   Beat in the milk and melted butter.

5   Break the chocolate into rough pieces and stir into the mixture.

6   Pour into the loaf tin.

7   Sprinkle the second amount of sugar and the other half of the cocoa powder over the top of the mixture.

8   Pour the milk over it, place the loaf tin in a shallow roasting tin and bake for 1 hour and 15 minutes. It is ready when the top feels crusty.

9   Carefully turn the whole thing out into a deep serving dish and eat it with cream while still hot.

NB. You can replace the dark chocolate with white chocolate if you prefer, or do a mixture of the two.

Old engine oil has a more refined taste than fresh. When engine oil is fresh it is more like caramel which doesn't go at all well with soil (not bad with fried ants though).

"'A plate of soil with engine oil's
A super recipe.
(I hardly need to mention that it's practically free.)'"

from
JAMES AND
THE GIANT PEACH

79

Going to Norway

Ever since I first saw her, Bestemama was terrifically ancient. She was a white-haired wrinkly-faced old bird who seemed always to be sitting in her rocking-chair, rocking away and smiling benignly at this vast influx of grandchildren who barged in from miles away to take over her house for a few hours every year.

Bestepapa was the quiet one. He was a small dignified scholar with a white goatee beard, and as far as I could gather, he was an astrologer, a meteorologist and speaker of ancient Greek. Like Bestemama, he sat most of the time quietly in a chair, saying very little and totally overwhelmed, I imagine, by the raucous rabble who were destroying his neat and polished home. The two things I remember most about Bestepapa were that he wore black boots and that he smoked an extraordinary pipe. The bowl of his pipe was made of meerschaum clay, and it had a flexible stem about three feet long so that the bowl rested on his lap.

Bestemama and Bestepapa (and Astri)

All the grown-ups including Nanny, and all the children even when the youngest was only a year old, sat down around the big oval dining-room table on the afternoon of our arrival, for the great annual celebration feast with the grandparents, and the food we received never varied. This was a Norwegian household, and for Norwegians the best food in the whole world is fish. And when they say fish, they don't mean the sort of thing you or I get from a fishmonger. They mean *fresh fish*, fish that has been caught no more than twenty-four hours before and has never been frozen or chilled on a block of ice. I agree with them that the proper way to prepare fish like this is to poach it, and that is what they do with the finest specimens. And Norwegians, by the way, always eat the skin of the boiled fish, which they say has the best taste of all.

So naturally this great celebration feast started with fish. A massive fish, a flounder as big as a tea-tray and as thick as your arm was brought to the table. It had nearly black skin on top which was covered with brilliant orange spots, and it had, of course, been perfectly poached. Large white hunks of this fish were carved out and put on to our plates, and with it we had hollandaise sauce and boiled new potatoes. Nothing else. And by gosh, it was delicious.

As soon as the remains of the fish had been cleared away, a tremendous craggy mountain of home-made ice-cream would be carried in. Apart from being the creamiest ice-cream in the world, the flavour was unforgettable. There were thousands of little chips of crisp burnt toffee mixed into it (the Norwegians call it *krokan*), and as a result it didn't simply melt in your mouth like ordinary ice-cream. You chewed it and it went crunch and the taste was something you dreamed about for days afterwards.

This great feast would be interrupted by a small speech of welcome from my grandfather, and the grown-ups would raise their long-stemmed wine glasses and say 'skaal' many times throughout the meal.

Krokan Ice-Cream

You will need:

kitchen foil
baking tray
frying pan
rolling pin
polythene bag

25g butter
75g almonds, skinned
and coarsely chopped
150g sugar
1 litre tub of good quality
vanilla ice cream

Serves 4–6

What you need to do:

This will keep for a couple of days before the Krokan begins to go soft.

1   Make the Krokan first. Lightly grease a piece of kitchen foil placed on a baking try.

2   Mix the butter, almonds and sugar in a heavy frying pan.

3   Place over a moderate heat and stir all the time, taking care that it doesn't burn.

4   When it's a good golden colour, pour the mixture onto the greased kitchen foil.

5   Allow to cool completely.

6   Place in a polythene bag and lightly crush into small pieces with a rolling pin.

7   Soften the ice-cream and then stir in the crushed Krokan until thoroughly mixed.

8   Place the ice-cream mixture back into the freezer until it is frozen again.

A perfect summer cooler

Stickjaw for

You will need:

piping bag and nozzle
baking sheet lined with
baking parchment
wire rack

2 egg whites
a pinch of salt
100g sugar
1 packet old-fashioned
treacle toffees
(e.g. Harrogate toffees or any
other hard toffee sweet)
with wrappers removed
food colouring

Serves 10–12

What you need to do:

1 Preheat oven to 140°C/gas mark 1.

2 Whisk the egg whites and salt to the texture of stiff snow.

3 Then gradually whisk in the sugar until the mixture is very stiff and shiny.

4 Place the meringue mixture into the piping bag with nozzle.

5 Pipe a little meringue onto the lined sheet. Rest a toffee on top and continue to pipe as you would for an ordinary meringue, making sure that each toffee is well covered.

6 Repeat until all the meringue is used up.

7 Bake for approx. 1 hour until dry and crisp and then cool on a wire rack.

NB. You can colour the meringue by adding a few drops of food colouring when whisking in the last amount of sugar.

Talkative Parents

Perfect for a midnight feast or a super present

Wonka's Whipple-scrumptious Fudgemallow Delight

You will need:

saucepan
1 adult

*large bowl of your
favourite ice cream
ready in the fridge*
60g dark chocolate
1 Cadbury's Crunchie
60g butter
80g dark brown sugar
150ml double cream
8 marshmallows

What you need to do:

1. Break the chocolate and the Crunchie into large chunks and set to one side.

2. In a saucepan, over a low heat, melt together the butter, sugar and cream.

3. Stir until all the sugar is dissolved and then turn the heat up and continue stirring for 10 minutes. Be careful, as it gets very hot and can splutter. Use a very long wooden spoon or a tall adult with a long arm.

4. Turn the heat down again, and get your bowl of ice-cream from the fridge.

5. Put the marshmallows, chocolate and Crunchie into the saucepan, stir around once and pour over your ice-cream.

NB. You can keep the leftover sauce in the fridge and reheat in the microwave.

"Wonka's Whipple-scrumptious Fudgemallow Delight!" cried Grandpa George. 'It's the best of them all! You'll just love it!'

Hot Frogs

You will need:

pencil
cardboard
pastry brush
pair of scissors or
Stanley knife
baking sheet

250g ready-made puff pastry
3–4 Granny Smith apples
(average sized so that when
cut in half they will fit
inside the template)
1 jar mincemeat or 200g
raisins soaked in orange juice
1 egg yolk, lightly beaten with
1 tbsp (15ml) of milk
(for egg wash)

For Eyes
12 raisins soaked in orange juice
1 tbsp (15ml) plain flour
1 carton of custard coloured
with a few drops of
green food colouring

Serves 6–7

What you need to do:

*The raisins will have to be soaked in the orange
juice for a couple of hours.*

1   Using your imagination, make your own
    template of a frog, measuring 13.5x13cm
    approx.

2   Preheat oven to 200°C/gas mark 6.

3   Roll out the puff pastry to the thickness of
    a two-pence coin.

4   With your template cut as many frogs as
    possible, approx. 6–7.

5   With a fork gently prick the frog's bellies
    several times.

6   Cut the apples in half vertically.

Perfect for Halloween

7 With a melon-scoop or teaspoon, scoop out the core and seeds.

8 Fill each apple hollow with a generous teaspoon of mincemeat or orange-soaked raisins.

9 Egg-wash the pastry frogs using a pastry brush.

10 Place the apples cut-side-down on the belly of each frog.

11 Position their eyes using the 12 raisins.

12 Lightly dust a baking sheet with flour and place the frogs on it.

13 Bake in the oven for approx. 15–20 minutes or until the pastry is risen and golden in colour.

14 Serve on a pool of warm green custard.

Grobswitchy Cake

You will need:

bowl
mixing bowl
electric whisk
20cm non-stick cake tin

4 tbsp (60ml) soft brown sugar
1 tsp (5ml) ground cinnamon
250g butter
150g caster sugar
2 eggs
300g sour cream
210g plain flour
70g self-raising flour
1 tsp (5ml) bicarbonate of soda
1 cup chopped pecans
*2 tbsp (30ml) grobswitchies
(also known as amber
sugar crystals)*

Serves 8

What you need to do:

1 Heat oven to 170°C/gas mark 3.

2 Mix together soft brown sugar and cinnamon and put to one side.

3 In a mixing bowl, cream the butter and sugar until pale and fluffy.

4 Add the eggs one at a time, whisking after each addition.

"It is a little bit like mixing a cake," the BFG said. 'If you is putting the right amounts of all the different things into it, you is making the cake come out any way you want, sugary, splongy, curranty, Christmassy or grobswitchy. It is the same with dreams.'"

5   Stir in the sour cream. Sift the plain flour, self-raising flour and bicarbonate of soda in together.

6   Add half the mixture to the cake tin.

7   Sprinkle in half the sugar and cinnamon mix, half the chopped pecans and half the grobswitchies.

8   Add the other half of the cake mix and then sprinkle the rest of the cinnamon and sugar, pecans and grobswitchies on the top.

9   Put in oven and cook for 1–1½ hours, or until a skewer comes out clean.

10 Allow to cool for about 15 minutes and then eat with some cream while still warm.

11 This cake keeps well for about a week.

NB. Grobswitchies remain hard even when cooked, so be careful if you have false teeth!

Luminous Lollies for Eating in Bed at Night

You will need:

food processor
small plastic/disposable cups
cling film
plastic forks
plastic spoons
luminous paint
(the type you can paint on plastic)
paintbrush

1 large ripe mango, chopped
2 tbsp (30ml) icing sugar
1 tsp (5ml) lemon juice

Makes about 12

NB. You should prepare these well in advance as they need a whole night to freeze.

perfect
for a
midnight
feast

What you need to do:

1   Put all the ingredients into the food processor and whizz until smooth.

2   Fill the plastic cups to 1cm below the top with the mango mix. Cover with cling film and place in the freezer overnight.

3   Paint the prong end of the forks and the bowl end of the spoons to a third of the way up the handle. Allow to dry completely.

4   Take one of the plastic cups out of the freezer and snip the top off the cup all around the edge at 1cm intervals (you will need to work quite quickly here so that you get to eat the lolly before it melts!). Tear down from the bits you have snipped so that all the sides of the cup are down.

5   Carefully place the frozen mango on a board and slice into 2cm rounds.

6   Slip these over the non-painted bits of the spoons and forks, making sure the food doesn't touch the paint.

7   You can eat these straight away or cover and put back in the freezer for another night.

Strawberry Bonbons

On the way to school and on the way back we always passed the sweet shop. No we didn't, we never passed it. We always stopped.

You will need:

food processor
fine sieve
small saucepan
tray
non-stick baking parchment
1 adult
toothpicks

200g strawberries
100g granulated sugar
8 tbsp (120ml) water
¼ tsp (1.25ml) liquid glucose

Strawberries on their own are scrumdiddlyumptious too!

What you need to do:

1   Liquidize half of the strawberries and then push the purée through a very fine sieve, so that you don't have any seeds left.

2   Put the sugar, water and liquid glucose into a small saucepan and stir over a low heat until all the sugar is melted.

3   Turn the heat up and stop stirring.

4   While this is cooking make sure that the remainder of the strawberries are completely dry. Place a sheet of non-stick baking parchment onto a tray in preparation for the next stage.

5   When the sugar and water starts to turn golden (about 5 minutes), turn off the heat and stir in 2 tbsp of the puréed strawberry. Be very careful when you add the purée, as it will spit, and it is extremely hot.

6   Allow the mixture to cool for 10 minutes, and then put the whole strawberries onto toothpicks and dip into the caramel. Place on the non-stick baking parchment to cool. These will start weeping after about 15 minutes, so don't delay long before eating!

SUPER SLURPS

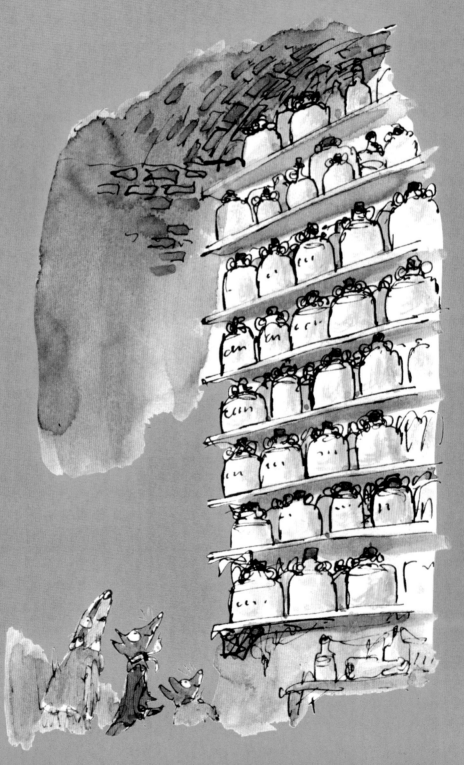

Bean's secret cider cellar

Mr Fox laughed and began pulling more bricks out of the wall. When he had made a biggish hole, he crept through it. Badger and the Smallest Fox followed him in.

They found themselves in a vast, damp, gloomy cellar.

'This is it!' cried Mr Fox.

'This is *what*?' said Badger. 'The place is empty.'

'Where are the turkeys?' asked the Smallest Fox, staring into the gloom. 'I thought Mr Bean was a turkey man.'

'He is a turkey man,' said Mr Fox. 'But we're not after turkeys now. We've got plenty of food.'

'Then what *do* we need, Dad?'

'Take a good look round,' said Mr Fox. 'Don't you see anything that interests you?'

Badger and the Smallest Fox peered into the half-darkness. As their eyes became accustomed to the gloom, they began to see what looked like a whole lot of big glass jars standing upon shelves around the walls. They went closer. They *were* jars. There were hundreds of them, and upon each one was written the word CIDER.

The Smallest Fox leaped high in the air. 'Oh, Dad!' he cried out. 'Look what we've found! It's cider!'

'Ex-actly,' said Mr Fox.

'Tremendous!' shouted Badger.

'Bean's Secret Cider Cellar,' said Mr Fox. 'But go carefully, my dears. Don't make a noise. This cellar is right underneath the farmhouse itself.'

'Cider,' said Badger, 'is especially good for Badgers. We take it as medicine – one large glass three times a day with meals and another at bedtime.'

'It will make the feast into a banquet,' said Mr Fox.

While they were talking, the Smallest Fox had sneaked a jar off the shelf and had taken a gulp. 'Wow!' he gasped. 'Wow-*ee*!'

You must understand that this was not the ordinary weak fizzy cider one buys in a store. It was the real stuff, a home-brewed fiery liquor that burned in your throat and boiled in your stomach.

'Ah-h-h-h-h-h!' gasped the Smallest Fox. 'This is some cider!'

'That is quite enough of that,' said Mr Fox, grabbing the jar and putting it to his own lips.

from FANTASTIC MR FOX

peach Juice

"And they all went over to the tunnel entrance and began scooping out great chunks of juicy, golden-coloured peach flesh."

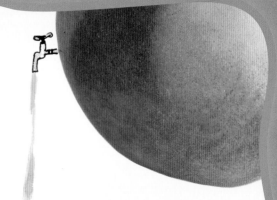

You will need:

food processor

400g tinned peaches in juice
425g tin mangoes
1 lemon, squeezed
or
6 fresh peaches, skinned
mango (hairless variety)
1 lemon squeezed.
ice cubes

Serves 4–6

What you need to do:

1   Liquidize all the ingredients, add ice cubes and serve immediately.

A perfect summer cooler

Liquid Chocolate Mixed by Waterfall

You will need:

rolling pin
saucepan
whisk

100g milk chocolate
100ml milk
1 Cadbury's Flake

Serves 1

What you need to do:

1. While the chocolate is still in its packaging, batter it with a rolling pin.

2. Put the chocolate bits into a saucepan and add the milk. Stir over a low heat until all the chocolate is melted.

3. Whisk the mixture to make it frothy and then pour it into the biggest mug you can find.

4. Use the Flake as a stirrer.

For a healthier version, use fat-free milk

Bean's Cider

You will need:

peeler
apple corer
food processor
fine-mesh sieve
small saucepan
strong arms

4 apples – a sweet variety
1 lime, squeezed
2 tbsp (30ml) light
muscovado sugar
1 cinnamon stick, broken
into 3 pieces
1 carton of apple juice

Serves 1

A perfect winter warmer

"Rat was perched upon the highest shelf in the cellar, peering out from behind a huge jar. There was a small rubber tube inserted into the neck of the jar, and Rat was using this tube to suck out the cider."

What you need to do:

1   Peel and core the apples.
2   Place in the food processor with lime juice and purée for 4 minutes.
3   Push through a very fine sieve into a small saucepan.
4   Add the muscovado sugar and the broken cinnamon stick.
5   Heat gently while stirring.
6   Push through a sieve again – if it is too thick, add some apple juice.
7   Pour into a mug and it's ready.

Fizzy Lifting Drinks

"'Oh, those are fabulous,' cried Mr Wonka. 'They fill you with bubbles ...'"

You will need:

cream soda
vanilla ice cream

Serves 1

A perfect birthday party drink

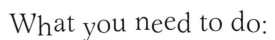

What you need to do:

1 Close all the doors so that you don't end up on the moon.

2 Pour cream soda into a glass.

3 Top with a giant scoop of vanilla ice cream.

4 Drink.

5 Burp.

The Three Best Friends

from THE GIRAFFE AND THE PELLY AND ME

To the monkey I gave a bag of Devil's Drenchers, those small fiery black sweets that one is not allowed to sell to children under four years old. When you have sucked a Devil's Drencher for a minute or so, you can set your breath alight and blow a huge column of fire twenty feet into the air. The Duke put a match to the Monkey's breath and shouted, 'Blow, Monkey, blow!' A sheet of orange flame shot up as high as the roof of the Grubber house and it was wonderful.

'I've got to leave you now,' I said. 'I must go and look after my customers in the shop.'

'We must go, too,' said the Giraffe. 'We have one hundred windows to clean before dark.'

I said goodbye to the Duke, and then one by one I said goodbye to the three best friends I had ever had. Suddenly, we all became very quiet and melancholy, and the Monkey looked as though he was about to cry as he sang me a little song of farewell'

Devil's Drenchers

You will need:

1 long wooden skewer
liquidizer or food processor

6 liquorice laces
9 strawberry laces
250g frozen raspberries
(you can freeze the berries
yourself or buy them frozen)
250g frozen cranberries
juice of 3 oranges
6 tbsp (90ml) icing sugar

Serves 1

What you need to do:

1   Tightly twist all the liquorice laces and 6 of the strawberry laces around the wooden skewer. Squish them together at the top.

2   Cut the remaining laces in half and drape over the top of the skewer. You will need to balance this in a glass while you make the quenching Drencher.

3   Place all remaining ingredients in the food processor or liquidizer and process until smooth.

4   Quickly spoon into another glass and spear in the laced skewer.

5   Eat or drink.

NB. This mixture can be sieved
if you don't like the seeds.

Perfect for Halloween

The great thing about a Devil's Drencher is that it is two recipes in one. When you first make it, you eat it with a spoon and if it melts before you finish it, it magically transforms into a delicious drink which you can suck through a straw.

frobscottle and whizzpoppers

Sophie opened her mouth, and very gently the BFG tipped the bottle forward and poured some of the fabulous frobscottle down her throat.

And oh gosh, how delicious it was! It was sweet and refreshing. It tasted of vanilla and cream, with just the faintest taste of raspberries on the edge of the flavour. And the bubbles were wonderful. Sophie could actually feel them bouncing and bursting all around her tummy. It was an amazing sensation. It felt as though hundreds of tiny people were dancing a jig inside her and tickling her with their toes. It was lovely.

'It's lovely,' she cried.

'Just wait,' said the BFG, flapping his ears.

Sophie could feel the bubbles travelling lower and lower down her tummy, and then suddenly, inevitably . . . the explosion came. The trumpets sounded and she too made the walls of the cavern ring with the sound of music and thunder.

'Bravo!' shouted the BFG, waving the bottle. 'You is very good for a beginner! Let's have some more!'

Frobscottle

"It's glummy!" he cried. 'I love it!'

You will need:

food processor
sieve
large jug

8 kiwi fruits, peeled
1 ½ limes, juice
200ml lemonade
100ml raspberry drinking yoghurt
300ml cream soda
1 tablet Redoxon effervescent
vitamin C (plain)

Makes 4–6 glasses

What you need to do:

1   In a food processor, liquidize the kiwis with the squeezed lime juice.

2   Push the pulp through a sieve into a large jug (a few seeds will escape, this doesn't matter).

3   Add the drinking yoghurt and mix.

4   Gradually mix in the lemonade.

5   Finally pour in the cream soda and mix.

6   Let the children drop the Redoxon tablet into the jug. Watch and then serve immediately.

NB. If you wish to substitute drinking yoghurt with ordinary yoghurt, add during step 1, when you liquidize the kiwis. The kiwis may also be substituted with tinned gooseberries in syrup (50g gooseberries = 1 kiwi fruit). A drop of green food colouring will improve the colour.

Blue Bubblers

You will need:

1 large glass
1 long wooden skewer

juice of 2 lemons
1 litre of sparkling water
caster sugar to taste
blue food colouring
6 blueberries
6 blackberries

Serves 1

So, it's the grown-ups' cocktail hour and you're not sure what to drink yourself.

Here is the answer.

A perfect birthday party drink

What you need to do:

1   Squeeze lemons, add the juice to the sparkling water and add sugar until it's sweet enough for you.

2   Add enough food colouring so that it is the perfect shade of blue (you won't need a lot).

3   Carefully thread the berries onto the skewer – alternating between the blueberries and the blackberries. The length of your skewer will depend on the height of your glass.

4   Place the skewer into the glass and let cocktail time officially begin . . .

Butterscotch

"'The Oompa-Loompas all adore it.
It makes them tiddly.'"

You will need:

large saucepan
large jug
whisk
cling film

25g butter
25g caster sugar
25g golden syrup
600ml fat-free milk
75ml natural yoghurt

Makes approx.
1 pint (3–4 mugs)

What you need to do:

1   In a saucepan, over a low heat, melt together the butter, sugar and golden syrup, stirring all the time until the sugar has dissolved (about 10 minutes). Add a little milk to the pan, then transfer to a jug.

2   Whisk in a little more milk, approx. 50ml followed by all the yoghurt.

3   Whisk in the remaining milk.

4   Cover with cling film. Chill before serving.

SPLENDIFEROUS MENU SUGGESTIONS

The repulsant snozzcumber

'Because you is guzzling human beans,' the BFG shouted. 'I is warning you not to do it and you is never taking the titchiest bit of notice.'

'In that case,' the Fleshlumpeater bellowed, 'I think we is guzzling *you* instead!'

The BFG grabbed the dangling rope and was hoisted out of the pit just in time.

The great bulging sack he had brought back with him from Giant Country lay at the top of the pit.

'What's in there?' the Queen asked him.

The BFG put an arm into the sack and pulled out a gigantic black and white striped object the size of a man.

'Snozzcumbers!' he cried. 'This is the repulsant snozzcumber, Majester, and that is all we is going to give these disgustive giants from now on!'

'May I taste it?' the Queen asked.

'Don't, Majester, don't!' cried the BFG. 'It is tasting of trogfilth and pigsquibble!' With that he tossed the snozzcumber to the giants below.

'There's your supper!' he shouted. 'Have a munch on that!' He fished out more snozzcumbers from the sack and threw them down. The giants below howled and cursed. The BFG laughed. 'It serves them right, left and centre!' he said.

'What will we feed them on when the snozzcumbers are all used up?' the Queen asked him.

'They is never being used up, Majester,' the BFG answered, smiling. 'I is also bringing in this sack a whole bungle of snozzcumber plants which I is giving, with your permissions, to the royal gardener to put in the soil. Then we is having an everlasting supply of this repulsant food to feed these thirstbloody giants on.'

'What a clever fellow you are,' the Queen said. 'You are not very well educated but you are really nobody's fool, I can see that.'

from THE BFG

Holiday Treats

Breakfast

The Hotel Breakfast

– have it brought to you in bed for a real treat!

Fruit salad is also a delicious breakfast treat – try it with mangoes, pineapples, melon, strawberries and oranges!

Teatime

Winkles for Tea

– if you're not too squeamish! Roald Dahl and his sisters thought this was a great treat!

If you don't fancy this, why not try toasted muffins or crumpets with butter and jam? Shrimps with salt, pepper and a squeeze of lemon are also very tasty on toast!

Lunch with Grandma

George's Marvellous Medicine Chicken Soup
*– this is very tasty with some
buttered bread to dip into it.*

Wait and see what it does to her . . .

Birthday Party

"Only once a year, on his birthday, did Charlie Bucket ever get to taste a bit of chocolate."

from CHARLIE AND THE CHOCOLATE FACTORY

Put everything out at the same time and you and your friends can take their pick!

Why not try a little bit of everything?

Drinks

Fizzy Lifting Drinks and Blue Bubblers

Treats

Sherbet Slurpers, Butter Gumballs, Nishnobblers, Strawberry Bonbons, Pishlets, Wonka's Nutty Crunch Surprise

Savoury snacks

Glumptious Globgobblers, Tummyticklers, Doc Spencer's Pie, Spitsizzlers, Crispy Wasp Stings on a Piece of Buttered Toast

Cake

Bruce Bogtrotter's Cake
– decorate it with candles and Smarties

Picnic

Here is a photograph of Roald Dahl and his family having a picnic while on holiday in Norway.

Glumptious Globgobblers
– very tasty cold and dipped in hummus!

Fresh Mudburgers
*– scrumdiddlyumptious cold – put them in a roll
and add ketchup and salad.*

Pishlets

Sherbet Slurpers
– yummy, easy to carry and will make you full of beans!

*Take lots of fresh fruit and
a big bottle of water too.*

Picnics can be thirsty work.

Summer Cooler

Peach Juice and
Krokan Ice-Cream

Winter Warmer

Boggis's Chicken with Bean's Cider and
Hot Ice-Cream for Cold Days for pudding

Mmmm Delumptious!

*Wrap up warm and get stuck into some hearty warming food
– you'll forget how bitter it is outside in no time.*

Halloween Dinner

"In fairy-tales, witches always wear silly black hats and black cloaks, and they ride on broomsticks. But this is not a fairy-tale. This is about REAL WITCHES."

from THE WITCHES

Starter

Green Pea Soup with crusty rolls

Main Course

Wormy Spaghetti with Hansel and Gretel Spare Ribs

*This would be delicious with a yummy green salad
or some tasty boiled peas!*

Pudding

Hot Frogs with warm green custard!

*Hot Frogs are also scrumdiddlyumptious
with natural yoghurt or double cream!*

Drinks

Devil's Drenchers

*If you don't fancy Hot Frogs, this would
also make a good pudding!*

Midnight Feast

Luminous Lollies for Eating in Bed at Night
and

Stickjaw for Talkative Parents
*so that the grown-ups can't tell
you to go to sleep!*

*Or be like Danny the Champion of the World
and his dad and make yourself some
sandwiches – any flavour you like!*

*NB. Don't forget to brush your teeth afterwards
and don't drink too many fizzy drinks or you'll
be whizzpopping all night!*

Perfect Presents

Strawberry Flavoured Chocolate Coated Fudge

Butter Gumballs

Stickjaw for Talkative Parents – *take them by surprise!*

Hair Toffee to Make Hair Grow on Bald Men –
you don't have to be bald to enjoy this tasty treat!

Hornets Stewed in Tar

The Magic Green Crystal

Nishnobblers

*All these treats will make brilliant presents.
Put them in a swanky box, tie a ribbon round it
and you've got a perfect (and tasty) gift!*

*You could make your own cards too.
Roald Dahl loved receiving home-made cards.*

My Splendiferous Menu Suggestions

Make up your own menus and note them down on the next pages. You can use recipes from this book, your own recipes, or a mixture of both!

My Splendiferous Menu Suggestions

FASCINATING

Roald Dahl liked his bacon sliced as thin as tissue paper and he loved the smell of bacon frying. Scrummdiddlyumptious!

Roald Dahl's dog, Chopper, used to sit on the arm of his chair during meals and at the end he would be rewarded with some Smarties.

The Enormous Crocodile's favourite food is children – but does he ever get to eat any?

Roald Dahl was famous in Great Missenden, the village where he lived, for growing giant onions!

Roald Dahl thought foie gras, mussels and snails were very tasty treats!

When a meal was ready, Roald Dahl would call everyone to the table by saying "Nosebags on!" or "Grub's up!"

Roald Dahl adored caviar. Caviar is sturgeon eggs – a sturgeon is a kind of fish.

FOODIE FACTS

In MATILDA, Miss Trunchbull forces Bruce Bogtrotter to eat a whole chocolate cake!

The little girl in THE PORCUPINE spends all her pocket money on Raspberry Creams.

Roald Dahl always kept a big jar of wine gums by his bed!

Roald Dahl was particularly partial to broad beans.

Roald Dahl had a habit of having pink milk for breakfast.

In DANNY THE CHAMPION OF THE WORLD, Danny and his dad go to Hazell's Wood to poach pheasants.

Roald Dahl's favourite type of shop was a fishmonger – he simply adored eating fresh fish.

As a child, Roald's favourite sweets were sherbet suckers.

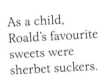

GLOSSARY

Arborio rice
an Italian rice named after the town where it is grown

Baking parchment
a non-stick paper used to line tins or trays to stop things from sticking to the tin. It is different to greaseproof paper because you don't have to grease it before you use it

Bubble wrap
special plastic wrapping to protect breakable things that was invented by accident in 1957 by two engineers. Also good for making Nishnobblers!

Capers
a pickled olive-green flower-bud. In Spain, capers are eaten as an alternative to olives

Caster sugar
very fine white sugar – perfect for meringues!

Caster
Sugar

Citric acid
a natural food preservative that is often added to soft drinks. It is found naturally in fruits like lemons and limes

"As I am telling you before, I know exactly what words I am wanting to say, but somehow or other they is always getting squiff squiddled around"

from THE BFG

Cream of tartar

is the common name for potassium hydrogen tartrate, which is an acid salt. Sounds nasty, but it isn't! It is a natural raising agent and often used in cooking. It is important to follow the recipe carefully

Demerara sugar

a special kind of sugar and it is usually brown, which is the natural colour of cane sugar. It is called Demerara because it originally came from the Demerara Colony in Guyana. Now, most of it comes from Mauritius

Evaporated milk

this is milk with most of the water removed from it. It comes in cans and keeps for much longer than fresh milk

Effervescent
fizzy

Liquid Glucose

which is sometimes called glucose syrup, is a clear, thick syrup that is often used in recipes for sweet treats. You can buy it in supermarkets and in chemists.

Garnish

food used to decorate a recipe or to make it taste better. This can be anything from a bit of salad to herbs sprinkled on top to a curl of lemon or orange zest – whatever you like as long as it's not poisonous!

Muscovado sugar

a dark brown sticky sugar with a strong flavour of molasses

GLOSSARY

Oasis
a squidgy foam that retains moisture. It is used to make flower arrangements with the stems stuck into the foam. You can buy it in florist's shops

Pastry brush
a special brush for using on pastry to coat it with butter, milk, oil or egg so that it doesn't burn and goes nice and crispy

Palette knife
a blunt knife with a flexible blade that is specially designed for spreading substances onto surfaces, like icing on a cake

Seasoned flour
plain flour mixed with a little salt and freshly ground black pepper

Pyrex bowl
heatproof glass bowl

Shucked
something that has had its shell or natural covering taken off it

Rasher
slice (used when talking about bacon)

Stanley knife

a sharp knife with a short blade which can be put inside the handle when it is not being used. The blade can be replaced when it is blunt

Skewer

a thin metal or wooden stick used to hold small pieces of food together while grilling. Wooden skewers must be soaked in water if you are going to use them on a grill – otherwise they will burn! They are usually made from bamboo

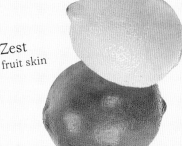

Sugar thermometer

a thermometer specially designed to check the temperature of sugar when you are making sweets. A sugar thermometer can also be used to measure the temperature of oil when deep frying. Be careful not to burn yourself as sugar gets very, very hot

Suet

a type of hard fat which is taken from around the kidneys of animals like sheep and cows. You can buy it in supermarkets and butcher's shops

Vermicelli

a sort of pasta that is long and thin, like spaghetti, but thinner. The name comes from the Italian for little worms!

Zest
fruit skin

THE
ROALD DAHL
FOUNDATION

There's more to Roald Dahl than great stories ...

Did you know that royalties from this book go to help the work of the Roald Dahl Foundation?

The Roald Dahl Foundation funds and supports specialist paediatric Roald Dahl nurses throughout the UK, caring for children with epilepsy, blood disorders and acquired brain injury. It also provides practical help for children and young people who have many different kinds of medical problems associated with the brain and blood, through grants to UK hospitals and charities as well as to individual children and their families.

www.roalddahlfoundation.org

charity no. 1004230